HARMONIZING SUCCESS

The Business Owner's Guide to Life Balance

LITRA SIMMS

Business Pledge for Life Balance

I, ______________________, as a business owner understand the importance of maintaining a work-life balance throughout my entrepreneurial endeavors. To ensure success and well-being I make the following promises:

1. **Prioritize Balance:** I will strive to maintain a balance between my work commitments and personal life.
2. **Embrace Realistic Expectations:** Recognizing that balance is ever-evolving I am prepared to adapt to changes and overcome challenges.
3. **Set Clear Boundaries:** I will establish boundaries between work and personal life to ensure both areas flourish.
4. **Value Self-Care:** I will allocate time for self-care, well-being, health, and mindfulness practices that contribute to my overall wellness.
5. **Optimize Time Management:** By prioritizing tasks based on their impact and utilizing the 80/20 principle for efficiency along with delegating when necessary.
6. **Leverage Technology Mindfully:** Using technology as a tool to boost productivity and connections while avoiding being overwhelmed by distractions.
7. **Cultivating a Supportive Network:** Seeking advice, mentorship, and encouragement from entrepreneurs, friends, and family members.
8. **Adapt and Thrive:** Integrating my interests into my business journey to enhance both aspects of my life.
9. **Regularly Evaluate and Celebrate:** Viewing change as an opportunity, for growth and demonstrating resilience when faced with challenges.

By committing to this promise my goal is to create a business while also prioritizing a satisfying lifestyle. I recognize that my path is continuous and with every move I make I draw nearer to realizing my equilibrium, in life.

Signature ______________________ **Start Date** ______________________

Completion Date ______________________ **Review/Reflection Date** ______________________

HARMONIZING SUCCESS

The Business Owner's Guide to Life Balance

TABLE OF CONTENTS

This guide aims to offer tips, real-world instances, and actionable advice for entrepreneurs to attain and sustain a work-life balance while effectively running their businesses. By understanding the significance of balance and putting these tips into practice, business owners can enjoy both their personal and professional spheres.

CHAPTER 1

Introduction

THE MYTH OF THE CONSTANT
In the fast-paced realm of business, the idea of hard work is commonly glorified. We aim to dispel this notion and present an approach to attaining success without compromising our health and happiness.

THE IMPORTANCE OF LIFE BALANCE FOR BUSINESS OWNERS
As a business owner, it's important to consider the advantages of keeping a life such as boosting creativity, making better decisions, and taking care of your health.

Chapter 1: Introduction
Worksheet Title: Unveiling the Myth of Constant Grind
Myth Reflections

- Share your reflections on the culture of business. How it has influenced you personally and in your work. Point out moments in your life where you
- have experienced the expectation to adhere to this perception.

Personal Definition

- Share your perspective on what it means to find balance in life.
- List the advantages you expect to experience by adopting a rounded lifestyle.

You can write your answers here...

You can write your answers here...

CHAPTER 2

Defining Life Balance as a Business Owner

UNDERSTANDING THE ELEMENTS OF LIFE BALANCE

Discover the essence of achieving life balance based on your situation. Explore the aspects of involving work, personal time, relationships, and self-care.

IDENTIFYING PERSONAL AND PROFESSIONAL PRIORITIES

Discover how to recognize and rank your individual and career objectives. Acquire perspectives on connecting your aspirations with your core beliefs.

Chapter 2: Defining Life Balance as a Business Owner
Worksheet Title: Balance Assessment

Wheel of Life

- Start by sketching a circle and splitting it into sections that symbolize aspects of your life such as work, family, and health.
- Assess your level of contentment in each category on a scale from 1 to 10. Take a moment to contemplate the harmony among them.

Priority Alignment

- Can you share the five things that matter the most to you personally in your professional life? Take a moment
- to reflect on whether the things you do every day match up with what you consider important.

YOUR NAME: ______________________________

DATE: ___________________________

EXAMPLE

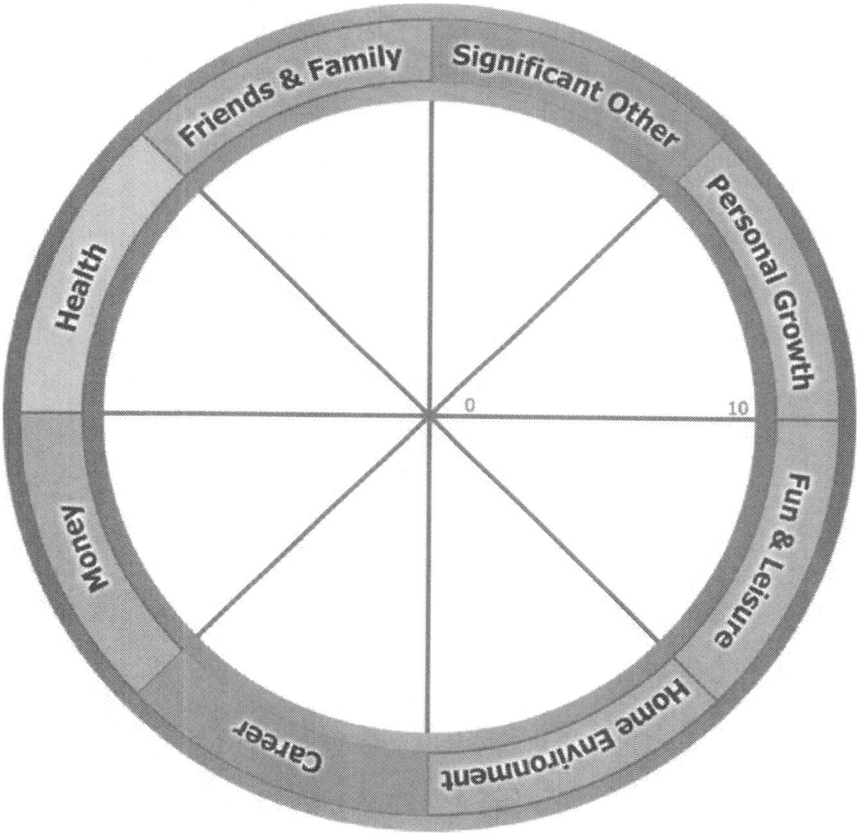

COMPLETE THE WHEEL

1. **Review the 8 Wheel Categories - think briefly what a satisfying life might look like for you in each area.**
2. **Next, draw a line across each segment that represents your satisfaction score for each area.**
   - Imagine the center of the wheel is 0 and the outer edge is 10
   - Choose a value between 1 (very dissatisfied) and 10 (fully satisfied)
   - Now draw a line and write the score alongside (see example above)

IMPORTANT: Use the FIRST number (score) that pops into your head, not the number you think it *should* be!

You can write your answers here...

You can write your answers here...

CHAPTER 3

The Impact of Imbalance

BURNOUT AND ITS CONSEQUENCES
Explore the risks associated with burnout, identify its symptoms, and understand how it can affect your well-being. Learn about methods to avoid burnout and bounce back from its effects.

STRAINED RELATIONSHIPS AND SOCIAL ISOLATION
Balancing the demands of work and personal life can put a strain on relationships which can potentially lead to feelings of isolation. Discover ways to nurture connections while striving for your goals.

DIMINISHED CREATIVITY AND PRODUCTIVITY
Discover how imbalance in your life can suppress your abilities and limit your effectiveness. Learn ways to nurture creativity and enhance your productivity.

Chapter 3: The Impact of Imbalance
Worksheet Title: Unpacking Imbalance Effects
Burnout Signs
Recognize any indications of burnout that you have personally felt or observed.
Make a note of methods to avoid or deal with these signs going forward.
Relationship Assessment
- Think about how stress from work can affect your relationships.

- Draft a letter to someone you care about sharing your dedication to finding a balance in life.

Creativity and Productivity Check:

- Think about moments when a lack of balance in your work impacted your ability to be creative and productive.
- Come up with ideas for things you can do to foster creativity and improve how efficiently you work.

You can write your answers here...

You can write your answers here...

You can write your answers here...

CHAPTER 4

Crafting Your Vision of Life Balance

CLARIFYING YOUR BUSINESS GOALS
Express your business goals clearly and precisely. This section assists you in establishing objectives while taking into account how they may affect your life.

ENVISIONING YOUR IDEAL LIFESTYLE
Dive into the journey of visualizing the kind of life you want. Discover how to blend your career goals, with your aspirations, for a rounded lifestyle.

SETTING REALISTIC EXPECTATIONS
Keep in mind that achieving balance doesn't always mean maintaining stability. Learn to embrace flexibility and adaptability while working towards your objectives.

Chapter 4: Crafting Your Vision of Life Balance
Worksheet Title: The Vision Mapping
Step 1: Define Your Business Goals

- Please outline the three goals you have for your business in the year.
- Explain how reaching these objectives would make a difference, in both your business operations and personal life.

Step 2: Envision Your Ideal Lifestyle

- Can you share what your perfect daily schedule looks like, one that allows for a mix of work and personal activities?
- What are some of the activities you enjoy doing to find satisfaction?

Step 3: Setting Realistic Expectations

- Think about the obstacles you can encounter when trying to find a balance.
- Write down some tactics you can use to tackle these hurdles.

You can write your answers here...

You can write your answers here...

You can write your answers here...

CHAPTER 5

Time Management and Prioritization

THE 80/20 PRINCIPLE FOR BUSINESS OWNERS

Utilize the 80/20 rule to pinpoint tasks that bring about the outcomes. Apply efficient time management strategies to concentrate on what counts.

DELEGATING AND OUTSOURCING TASKS

Discover the benefits of delegating tasks to ease your workload and support your team. Gain insights on outsourcing responsibilities to boost productivity.

MASTERING THE ART OF SAYING NO

Learn how to politely decline opportunities that don't match your priorities. Develop the skills to safeguard your time and energy.

Chapter 5: Time Management and Prioritization

Worksheet Title: Prioritization Matrix

Task Assessment

- Please share the tasks and projects you are currently working on.
- Classify each task as either "Important," "Not Urgent," or "Not Important."

80/20 Application

- Focus on the tasks that lead to the majority of your desired results.
- Explore ways to delegate or streamline the remaining tasks.

You can write your answers here...

You can write your answers here...

CHAPTER 6

Boundaries and Work-Life Separation

CREATING PHYSICAL AND MENTAL BOUNDARIES

Make sure you set up boundaries between your work life and personal life to avoid them overlapping. Put in place methods to separate your workspaces and schedules.

DESIGNING AN EFFECTIVE WORKSPACE

Create a workspace that encourages concentration and innovation while reducing interruptions. Delve into designing concepts for a working atmosphere.

UNPLUGGING AND RECHARGING

Understand the significance of taking breaks from work to rejuvenate. Explore methods for relaxation and tactics for upholding a balance between work and personal life.

Chapter 6: Boundaries and Work-Life Separation

Worksheet Title: Boundary Building

Boundary Visualization:

- Sketch out a boundary that reflects your desired balance between work and personal life.
- Note down behaviors or activities that support upholding this divide.

Workspace Reflection

- Can you talk about where you work and how it affects your work-life balance?
- What are three adjustments you could implement to foster a setting?

You can write your answers here...

You can write your answers here...

CHAPTER 7

Nurturing Your Well-Being

THE IMPORTANCE OF PHYSICAL HEALTH

Make sure to take care of your body by focusing on exercise, eating well, and getting rest. Recognize how your physical health and your work are interconnected.

CULTIVATING MENTAL AND EMOTIONAL RESILIENCE

Cultivate a mindset to overcome obstacles and setbacks. Dive into mindfulness practices and strategies for managing emotions to improve your wellness.

INCORPORATING MINDFULNESS AND MEDITATION

Utilize mindfulness and meditation to enhance self-awareness and reduce stress. Explore how these techniques can have an effect on your business endeavors.

Chapter 7: Nurturing Your Well-Being

Worksheet Title: Well-Being Check-In

Physical Health

- How would you rate your workout regimen? What goal are you aiming to achieve?
- Can you share three meals that you like and intend to include in your eating plan?

Mental and Emotional Resilience

- Think about a time when you faced a situation and share how you handled it.
- Write down an activity you can do when you are feeling stressed out.

Mindfulness and Meditation

- Select a mindfulness routine to engage in every day for the week.
- Reflect on how practicing mindfulness influences your concentration and emotional state.

You can write your answers here...

You can write your answers here...

You can write your answers here...

CHAPTER 8

Leveraging Technology for Balance

PRODUCTIVITY TOOLS FOR BUSINESS OWNERS

Discover a variety of productivity tools powered by technology that can enhance efficiency in your business operations. Find out how to leverage technology to increase productivity without increasing effort.

USING SOCIAL MEDIA WISELY

Explore the realm of media without letting it consume all your time and energy. Create tactics to uphold a presence while juggling responsibilities.

AVOIDING DIGITAL OVERWHELM

Avoid getting overwhelmed by the realm by adopting techniques to handle emails, alerts, and internet diversions. Cultivate a connection with technology.

Chapter 8: Leveraging Technology for Balance

Worksheet Title: Technology Audit

Digital Overwhelm Evaluation

- Could you please share the technology tools? Platforms you rely on for your job?
- Are there any sources of overload or distractions that you encounter during your workday?

Technology Optimization

- Select a tech-related issue that you're dealing with and think of ways to solve it.
- Try out a method to improve how you handle your interactions.

You can write your answers here...

You can write your answers here...

CHAPTER 9

Building a Support System

SEEKING MENTORSHIP AND GUIDANCE

Understanding the importance of mentorship on your path an an entrepreneur is key. Discover ways to connect with and cultivate relationships with mentors who offer perspectives.

NURTURING RELATIONSHIPS WITH FAMILY AND FRIENDS

Discover ways to stay connected with your loved ones even when you are swamped with your routine. Cultivate empathy and encouragement from those dearest to you.

JOINING BUSINESS-OWNER NETWORKS AND COMMUNITIES

Uncover the advantages of connecting with business owners. Seek out. Form groups that provide perspectives, teamwork, and a feeling of camaraderie.

Chapter 9: Building a Support System

Worksheet Title: Support Network Assessment

Current Support System

- Identify the people or organizations that offer assistance during your business venture.
- Evaluate the impact of each support network on a scale from 1 to 10.

Mentorship Exploration

- Find the areas where you could use some help or advice.
- Look into mentors or advisors who match what you are looking for.

You can write your answers here...

You can write your answers here...

CHAPTER 10

Flexibility and Adaptability

EMBRACING CHANGE IN BUSINESS AND LIFE
Discover how to adapt to change and unpredictability with strength. Embrace a perspective that sees obstacles as chances for development.

ADJUSTING YOUR STRATEGIES AS NEEDED
Know when it's necessary to shift or tweak your business tactics. Cultivate the skill to make informed choices in response to evolving situations.

FINDING OPPORTUNITIES IN CHALLENGES
Transform obstacles into opportunities for achievement. Discover inspiring stories of business owners who turned hardships into creativity.

Chapter 10: Flexibility and Adaptability
Worksheet Title: Embracing Change

Change Assessment

- Share any developments in your industry or the business landscape.
- Assess the advantages and hurdles that come with these shifts.

Strategies for Adaptation

- Find aspects of your business that may need modifications because of shifts.
- Come up with strategies to adjust and succeed in circumstances.

You can write your answers here...

You can write your answers here...

CHAPTER 11

Work-Life Integration

ALIGNING YOUR PASSIONS WITH YOUR BUSINESS
Uncover the potential of connecting your interests with your endeavors. Achieve an integration of your hobbies and your career.

FINDING MOMENTS OF JOY IN DAILY TASKS
Bring happiness and purpose into your work tasks. Discover the art of enjoying the process and acknowledging wins as you progress.

CREATING SYNERGY BETWEEN YOUR WORK AND PERSONAL LIFE
Discover methods to blend your work and personal interests harmoniously. Aim for a life where each facet enhances and complements the other.

Chapter 11: Work-Life Integration
Worksheet Title: Passion-Alignment Exercise

Passion Assessment

- Share your things to do in your time and what you enjoy.
- Think about how these activities connect with what you are working on in your business.

Passion Integration

- Consider incorporating your interests into your work to enhance your business endeavors.
- Generate innovative ideas that connect your projects with your hobbies and passions.

You can write your answers here...

You can write your answers here...

CHAPTER 12

The Continuous Journey

EVALUATING AND ADJUSTING YOUR LIFE BALANCE REGULARLY
Finding Harmony Over Time - Recognize that achieving balance in life is a journey not a fixed destination. Regularly refine your strategies to maintain stability.

CELEBRATING YOUR ACHIEVEMENTS
Take time to acknowledge and celebrate your accomplishments, no matter how big or small. Practice gratitude for the progress you have made towards achieving balance.

EMBRACING LIFELONG LEARNING AND GROWTH
Foster a mindset of growth that emphasizes learning and self-improvement. Experience the satisfaction of evolving both as an entrepreneur and as an individual.

Chapter 12: The Continuous Journey
Worksheet Title: Balance Evaluation

Regular Evaluation

- Remember to assess your work-life equilibrium every quarter.
- Ponder on the strides you have taken since embarking on this path.

Milestone Celebration

- Outline three recent achievements whether significant or small.
- Explain how each achievement has influenced your general life harmony.

Lifelong Learning and Growth

- Select a life skill or field of knowledge for enhancement in the year.
- Chart out the actions you'll undertake to gain knowledge and improve in this domain.

You can write your answers here...

You can write your answers here...

You can write your answers here...

CHAPTER 13

Case Studies: Real-Life Examples of Business Owners and Their Paths to Balance

ENTREPRENEUR A: BALANCING A STARTUP AND FAMILY LIFE

- Balancing the phases of a business while cherishing moments with family.
- Approaching engaging family members in the adventure.
- Establishing limits to safeguard moments with those close to us.

ENTREPRENEUR B: SCALING A BUSINESS WHILE PRIORITIZING HEALTH

- Managing the obstacles of expansion while prioritizing one's health and happiness.
- Integrating activity, healthy eating, and adequate rest into the schedule of a busy business owner.
- Juggling responsibilities with taking care of oneself.

ENTREPRENEUR C: THRIVING IN A DYNAMIC AND EVER-CHANGING INDUSTRY

- Adjusting to changes in the industry while remaining committed to beliefs.
- Welcoming shifts and unpredictability as chances for development.
- Cultivating a mindset to handle obstacles with poise.

Chapter 13: Case Studies: Real-Life Examples of Business Owners and Their Paths to Balance

Worksheet Title: Case Study Reflection

Entrepreneur A, B, C Analysis

- Showcase the tactics employed by each entrepreneur to attain equilibrium.
- Pinpoint one lesson or perspective that you can incorporate into your own journey.

You can write your answers here...

You can write your answers here...

You can write your answers here...

CHAPTER 14

Conclusion

In this final chapter, as a business owner striving for a fulfilling life, we look back on the journey you have taken. We review the lessons you have learned, the changes you have embraced, and the accomplishments you have reached in both your personal spheres. Keep in mind that achieving work-life balance is a journey that never truly ends. As you progress, you have the resources and understanding to adapt and steer your course continually.

Chapter 14: Conclusion

Worksheet Title: Next Steps Planning

Reflection and Goal Setting

- Think about your experiences with the book and how you are managing your life now.
- Choose an objective to focus on each day, week, month, or year as you strive for balance in your life.

You can write your answers here...

CHAPTER 15

Additional Resources

Discover a selection of materials to assist you in maintaining a life as an entrepreneur. This collection comprises suggested readings, podcasts, web-based classes, and utilities that offer insights on business ownership, effective time management, personal wellness, and various other topics. Make use of these materials to expand your knowledge and advance your development outside the confines of this book.

You can write your answers here...

You can write your answers here...

You can write your answers here...

Reflections

1. **Balance is Key** – Success is about finding harmony between ambition and well-being.
2. **Prioritize Self-Care** – You can't pour from an empty cup. Nurture yourself to nurture your goals.
3. **Embrace Flexibility** – True success adapts and evolves with life's changes.
4. **Focus on Your 'Why'** – Understanding your purpose is the foundation for meaningful success.
5. **Celebrate Small Wins** – Progress is built on acknowledging and appreciating every step forward.
6. **Learn to Say No** – Boundaries are essential for maintaining balance and avoiding burnout.
7. **Invest in Relationships** – Genuine connections fuel personal and professional growth.
8. **Success is a Journey, Not a Destination** – Enjoy the process as much as the outcome.
9. **Growth Happens Outside Your Comfort Zone** – Embrace discomfort as a catalyst for success.
10. **Mindset Matters** – Cultivate a positive, resilient mindset to overcome obstacles.
11. **Align with Your Values** – True success is built on integrity and staying true to your core beliefs.
12. **Practice Gratitude** – A grateful heart attracts abundance and fosters a sense of fulfillment.
13. **Delegate and Trust** – You don't have to do it all yourself. Trust others to share the load.
14. **Rest and Recharge** – Success isn't sustainable without regular periods of rest and reflection.
15. **Know Your Limits** – Understanding when to push and when to step back is a vital part of success.
16. **Success is Personal** – Define success on your own terms, not by societal standards.
17. **Stay Open to Learning** – Every experience, good or bad, is an opportunity to learn and grow.
18. **Be Patient** – Great things take time; trust the process and give your efforts time to flourish.
19. **Surround Yourself with Positivity** – The energy and attitudes of those around you impact your success.
20. **Give Back** – True success includes using your achievements to uplift others and contribute to your community.

Challenge Questions

1. What does success truly mean to you, beyond material achievements?
2. How do you currently balance your personal and professional life, and where do you see room for improvement?
3. Are your goals aligned with your core values? How can you adjust if they aren't?
4. When was the last time you took time for self-care, and how did it affect your productivity?
5. What limiting beliefs are holding you back from reaching your full potential, and how can you overcome them?
6. How do you handle failure? Do you view it as a stepping stone toward success or a setback?
7. In what ways do you practice gratitude in your daily life? How could you incorporate more?
8. How do you prioritize your time, and are you investing enough in the things that truly matter?
9. Are there tasks or responsibilities you're holding onto that could be delegated to others?
10. How well do you set boundaries in both your personal and professional life?
11. What steps are you taking to nurture your relationships and build meaningful connections?
12. Do you regularly celebrate your progress or are you always focused on the next goal?
13. How do you handle stress and what techniques can you use to better manage it?
14. In what areas of your life do you feel out of balance, and what can you do to restore harmony?
15. How comfortable are you with stepping out of your comfort zone? What's one thing you could do today to challenge yourself?
16. How often do you reflect on your 'why,' and does it still resonate with your current goals?

Congratulations!

You have a book that delves into ways to maintain a balanced life as an entrepreneur. Keep in mind that sharing your experiences and perspectives will add richness to every chapter ensuring the book resonates with and benefits your business objectives.

Good luck with your life and business journey!

Discover More with the *Harmonizing Success* Podcast

If you're enjoying the insights and strategies in this book, I invite you to take the journey further with the *Harmonizing Success* podcast. Each episode is designed to complement the principles you're reading about, offering fresh perspectives, actionable tips, and inspiring conversations. Here's what you can expect:

- **Deep Dives:** Explore key topics from the book in greater detail with practical examples and expert advice.
- **Real Stories:** Hear from entrepreneurs, leaders, and wellness experts who have harmonized success in their lives.
- **Interactive Challenges:** Get involved with challenges and reflections to help you implement what you learn.
- **'Ask Litra':** Have questions? asklitra@litrasimms.com Tune in for answers to listener-submitted questions on balancing business, family, and personal growth.

Success isn't a destination—it's a journey. The podcast is here to walk with you every step of the way, providing guidance and encouragement as you balance ambition with well-being.

Subscribe today and start creating the harmony you deserve. Available wherever you listen to podcasts!